EMOTIONAL INTELLIGENCE 101

How Emotional Awareness
Can Change Your Life

By JOSHUA ELANS

Table of Contents

Introduction

Emotional intelligence (EI) or emotional quotient (EQ) stands for the ability of individuals to tune in with their own, and other people's emotions — to recognize them, above all. It also stands for one's capability to discriminate between different feelings and to use this information in thinking and acting.

Before we embark on the journey of learning about emotional intelligence, let's first tackle the question: why should you care? Why does EI matter?

Studies have found that raising one's emotional intelligence leads to a happier life. As you begin developing your EQ, you will begin to learn when to be happy and excited, and when to be sad or anxious, and how to react to the changing circumstances of life. Very few people let their feelings go unnoticed, until one day they find themselves trapped in a cocoon of unidentifiable feelings and even more mysterious emotional reactions.

If you find yourself saying "This is not who I am" the first time you unwillingly explode in anger towards your loved one, that's the first step on your journey to leading a more conscious and happy life, because emotionally intelligent people have the ability to control their mood to serve their purpose.

As you keep on reading the book, take a note that there is an important difference between learning about emotional intelligence and implementing the knowledge into your own life. Even though we start off with theory and the origins of the term, there are many practical examples and pieces of advice to help you start a new emotional routine today.

Chapter 1: Emotional Intelligence in Theory

What does leading a full and happy life mean nowadays? Paradoxically, in the modern society, where most people have their basic needs met, a fulfilling life requires more effort to attain than it did ever before.

Learning how to develop emotional intelligence will help you build stronger bonds with people close to you, focus on your work with more success, and take every open opportunity to share your potential with the world.

As you begin to develop your emotional intelligence, you will begin to learn when to be happy and excited, and when to be sad or anxious, and how to react to the changing circumstances of life. Very few people let their feelings go unnoticed, until one day they find themselves trapped in a cocoon of unidentifiable feelings and even more mysterious emotional reactions.

In the next few chapters, you will learn more about theory and practice behind Emotional intelligence: who are the theorists who introduced it, what it means to be emotionally intelligent and how you can make your first steps towards the awaken living.

The term itself became popular in the 1995 book "Emotional Intelligence", written by the author, psychologist, and science journalist Daniel Goleman. In this book, Goleman points out the importance of EI in shaping people's success and equals it with the importance of IQ. He goes even a step further and writes about methods for incorporating emotional skills training in school programs.

Howard Gardner introduced the idea that traditional types of intelligence, such as IQ, couldn't fully explain person's cognitive ability. Therefore, he was certain of the idea of both *interpersonal* (being able to understand intentions of the others) and *intrapersonal intelligence* (having the ability to understand oneself — our own feelings, motivations, fears, etc).

Regardless, the first person considered to be the first to use the term "emotional intelligence" was Wayne Payne in his 1985 doctoral thesis, *A Study of Emotion: Developing Emotional Intelligence.*

The first time the term "emotional quotient" was published was in 1987 Keith Beasley's article in British Mensa magazine, although Reuven Bar-On claims to have used the term in an unpublished version of his graduate thesis.

However, it was only with the publication of Goleman's book: *Emotional Intelligence - Why it can matter more than IQ* in 1995 that the term gained on popularity. With its best-selling status, the book reached a large audience worldwide. Additionally, Goleman followed this success with several popular publications around the same topic.

Emotional intelligence was put under the bright lights when first studies showed that people graded as highly emotional intelligent have greater job performance, mental health, and leadership skills. However, researchers speculate that this might be attributable to general intelligence and certain personal traits. Goleman's conclusion was that emotional intelligence accounts for 67% of what is regarded to be superior leadership performance, and mattered twice as much as one's technical expertise or IQ.

Some other studies, however, have found that emotional intelligence doesn't have as significant impact on leadership and managerial performance as Goleman had suggested, in cases where ability and personality are controlled for. In this case, general intelligence is correlated with leadership very closely.

Nevertheless, clues that emotional intelligence is not to be ignored when leadership and one's well-being is considered, influenced markers of emotional intelligence and methods for its development to become more widely coveted in the past decade. This also led to having more studies done in order to provide evidence to help dig deeper into neural mechanisms of emotional intelligence.

Chapter 2: Goleman's Models of Emotional Intelligence

At the time when Goleman first published "Emotional Intelligence: Why It Can Matter More than IQ" in 1995, it was considered that cognitive intelligence was the prominent type of intelligence. His work set the foundations for a global movement that claimed exactly the opposite.

Even though no one at the time denied the importance of emotional strength for social and professional success, Goleman attempted to answer some additional questions that could lead to higher satisfaction at work and at home. Among others: what can we change that will help our children fare better in life?

At the get-go, taking into account the role of genetic determinism, he approached emotional intelligence as a skill that can be learnt.

Goleman introduced so-called *mixed model* of emotional intelligence, which takes into account a wide array of skills that help effective leadership. His model answers a question that's in the title of his Harvard Business Review piece "What makes a leader?". According to his writing, five traits are at the very core of every leader's success:

1. Self-awareness
2. Self-regulation
3. Social-skills
4. Empathy
5. Motivation.

According to Goleman, in order to improve emotional intelligence, one has to start from number one, the self-awareness. This could be regarded as one's capacity to recognize oneself as separate from others and the environment.

As an example of how this affects leadership, Goleman writes that emotionally self-aware leaders are attuned to their inner "signals", they are able to recognize how their emotions influence their well-being and efficiency. Most importantly, they make their values part of their work — this leading to clear judgment and decision-making influenced by what they truly care for. According to Goleman, this brings about the ability to see the big picture, and approach it genuinely.

For him, being self-aware literally means being aware of how our emotional state affects our thinking, decision-making, and interactions. He also points out that different parts of our brains allow us to be aware of our physical and our mental worlds.

According to Goleman, there are three competencies associated with self-awareness:

1. **Emotional self-awareness**
2. **Accurate self-assessment**
3. **Self-confidence**.

Emotional Self-Awareness

As mentioned, Goleman argues that self-awareness can be developed. The question is how, and he proposes some initial steps available to anyone. For example, spending some time recognizing areas you need to develop and intentionally making an effort to develop or strengthen that aspect of yourself. In order to achieve this, you'll need to find answers to a few questions:

- What do you think your strengths are? What are you limitations?
- What do others think of you? Be open to hearing their feedback;
- Complete a formal assessment test. These could include a personality test, discovering your values, skills, and abilities.

Being aware of one's own feelings will not only help that person reflect on thoughts and reactions, but will also help them feel empathy towards others. Three aspects of awareness are acknowledgment, acceptance, and identification.

Acknowledging feelings, means to be able to correctly direct our attention to the most important information that surrounds us". Take for example negative emotions —
learning to detect them will help us find what is our body and mind trying to call attention to. By learning this, we take control over fixing the way we feel.

Self-awareness goes into detail: especially with negative feelings, psychologists stress the importance of identifying the feeling as specifically as possible. If you are feeling stressed now, what feelings preceded it? The more specific we describe feelings, the more success we will have in identifying the unmet emotional needs.

Naming the feelings helps build self-awareness for two reasons. People are conformists and fear the unknown. As soon as we label our feelings, we consciously make them known and familiar. This helps make them more easily manageable. Some research shows that when we label an emotion, we are using the upper part of our brains and moving the chemicals from our emotional to our reasoning brain, allowing us to access the ways we feel clearly.

Practices that will help you become more self-aware are simple and anyone can do them daily. Take, for example, keeping a diary — documenting your feelings will help you trace all those times when you felt certain way towards other people's actions, shifts in the environment, or the things you do regularly.

Writing down a list of your social roles and feelings attached to them will help you identify the strength and quality of connection to each of them. For example, what are your feelings towards the role of a sibling in your family? Are you joyous or anxious? Think of as many as possible.

Again, turn to your journal and predict how you will feel in an upcoming situation. Naming the feeling and putting it into a sentence (such as: "I may feel confused"), will help you get a hold of the situation.

Accurate Self-Assessment

Self-assessment stands for the process of looking at oneself in order to determine aspects that are important to a person's identity. Building self-awareness begins with self-assessment, and what follows is a motivated person who seeks information that will confirm his or her uncertain self-concept. Self-assessment, however, enables a person to check the accuracy of their current self-view, rather than improving it.

For this reason, in certain cases self-assessment may harm a person's self-concept through realizing their self-view does not align with an objective view in a certain situation. Once this happens, it also poses a positive challenge and an opportunity for improvement.

Self-Confidence

Simply put, self-confidence means to put trust and faith into oneself and one's engagement with the world. A person described as self-confident acts on opportunities, looks forward to new challenges and takes control if something goes astray.

Self-confidence builds up on successful experiences, and that's why psychologists stress the importance of formative years in childhood and adolescence. Positive self-belief is linked to the quality of one's relationships, body image, and physical health. Especially in adolescence, self-confidence is affected by race, ethnicity, body properties, gender and sexual identity and acceptance in social circles.

Even though self-confidence and self-esteem are thought to go hand in hand, it is possible for people to have high self-confidence, but low self-esteem. In the Western world, self-esteem is usually formed on achievement, while in the East it is based on being a good member of the family and community.

Ability Model and Trait Model of EI

Besides the mixed method, researchers also differentiate between the so-called *ability* emotional intelligence and t*rait* emotional intelligence.

Ability model

The first was developed by psychologists Peter Salovey and John Mayer in 2004, and its focus is on the individual's ability to gather and process emotional information from the environment and to navigate the social surrounding using it.

It, therefore, puts together four different types of ability into a single model:

1. **Emotional perception**

A majority of people has the ability to recognize other's emotions through facial expression, body language, pictures, voices, and so on. This ability also includes being capable of identifying one's own emotions.

Emotional perception has been at the root of emotional intelligence theory from the very beginning. Those who argue for the ability model often call forward the case of people with autism in order to explain the importance of emotional perception: the difficulty with learning social cues comes from their limited ability to recognize the emotions of others through facial expressions or body language.

2. Use of emotions

The second type of ability emphasized by the Ability Model relates to one's capacity to use emotions — one's own or other person's — to reach the desired goal. Decision-making and problem-solving asks for emotions to be considered, while a person in control of using them manages to act or make decisions based on the moods of themselves or other people. One example of this would be a child knowing the right time to ask a parent for a permission. A kid would not approach a touchy subject if a parent expresses anger, frustration or stress.

3. Understanding emotions

Emotions and the languages that communicate them are complex. While many people do have the ability to perceive and understand basic facial expressions, fewer are capable of understanding the variety of nuances of complex emotional relationships. Cases where emotions are not white and black, such as in times of divorce, when the outcome might bring sorrow and relief to the parted partners at the same time, some people might have a lower level of ability to understand the situation.

4. **Managing emotions**

The fourth ability relates to the question of whether one is capable of handling emotions in themselves and others. A person graded with high levels of emotional intelligence is expected to successfully manipulate their own feelings and those of others in order to achieve a certain outcome.

Even though emotional manipulation holds a negative tag, it serves very important purposes in almost all of our relationships. Take for example a school teacher who uses their own students' aspirations in terms of grades and performance results to motivate them to work harder. This helps both the student and the teacher to get the most of their experience and relationship.

According to Ability Model EI is measured by a series of problem-solving duties or tasks. This model sees emotional intelligence as *true or pure intelligence*, and, therefore, uses tests based on measuring cognitive IQ.

The problem-solving tasks are testing a person's competence on each of the four ability types, mentioned beforehand. Since the model is tightly linked with social mores, its evaluation is scored in a consensus fashion. The test is not objective, and for this reason, it is measured against a global sample of respondents as a way to determine whether a person adheres to social norms.

Contrary to Goleman's appreciation of the role our instincts play in emotional decision-making, the ability theory puts more demand on thinking. Therefore, its proponents believe that given characteristics are not the key factor determining levels of one's ability EI, as much as this is training. To them, high levels of emotional intelligence mean the person is capable of controlling and using their own and others emotions — emotions are a tool for achieving goals.

Trait model

Trait emotional intelligence was introduced in 2001 by K. V. Petrifies. This model looks at an individual's self-perceptions of their emotional abilities because these have an effect on person's behavior and thinking. Self-reporting, as it is sometimes thought of, resides completely in the perceptions of the individual. This makes it incredibly hard to measure objectively, but also hard to disprove.

Even though trait and ability model have their respected differences, they both contain core elements of the general definition of EI: the understanding of one's own emotions and regulation of others' emotions.

According to the Trait Model, the role of self-perception affects all awareness and regulation of one's own emotions. Going out of oneself, and recognizing and controlling the emotions of others is found in the recognition that many people are capable of understanding and affecting others in an almost effortless manner when they are "being themselves", or relying on their natural personality characteristics. Once an individual has the power to recognize and use their own emotions and the traits of their personality, they will be equipped to understand and influence the emotions of those they get in touch with.

In order to detect someone's Trait EI, the person has to perform a personality evaluation. Because it heavily relies on personality, some psychologists suggest that this model cannot serve as a measure of emotional intelligence. Others believe that EI is meant to be within the framework of cognitive-emotional ability, rather than plain personality attributes.

Among the aspects of personalities that relate to EI and are measured within the Trait Model are: adaptability and flexibility, assertiveness and assertive communication, emotion expression, emotion management, emotion perception (of self and others), impulsiveness, self-esteem, self-motivation, social awareness, stress management, trait empathy, happiness, and optimism.

Trait model of EI takes into consideration the complexity of various traits and their representation in different circumstances and environments. Characteristics that make someone successful at work, could possibly make them less successful in some other roles, for instance as a spouse or a parent.

As previously mentioned, evaluating the Trait Model of EI using self-reports has been a long-time practice. These evaluations include measures of personality traits, rather than cognitive characteristics. Distributed globally, the psychometric properties of the Trait questionnaire have been investigated in numerous countries and scores have been found to be normally distributed and reliable worldwide. Additionally, as researchers compared the Trait Emotional Intelligence Questionnaire with other EI tests, they found it to be notably valid scientifically.

Constant iterations have led researchers to develop better methods for self-reporting and conducting subjective evaluations in a reliable fashion, but even today self-reporting is often poorly received by the scientific community. One of the most relevant reasons why this is so, is that self-reporting is susceptible to faking and crafting socially desirable responses.

Chapter 3: How to improve your Emotional Intelligence?

As mentioned previously, being emotionally intelligent will show in your life as the ability to identify and control your own emotions and reactions, as well as to clearly communicate how we feel to others. It is widely believed that EI can be a key to success in your life and sometimes — especially in your career where it can matter more than technical knowledge and expertise.

Emotional intelligence can be learned — it takes time, effort and disciplined work on oneself to attain it. Once you make progress, the award will be enormous — fulfilling relationships, better work results and self-love and appreciation.

Goleman divided emotional intelligence into 'Personal' and 'Social' competencies, which splits into two questions: 'How do we manage ourselves?' and 'How do we manage relationships with others?'. According to this, we are now going to look at how you can develop both aspects.

Improving interpersonal skills

We use interpersonal skills to interact with others — they help us build strong and meaningful relationships, something that every social being yearns for. From what you have learnt about emotional intelligence so far, you can notice that interpersonal skills lie at that very center of emotional intelligence.

They ask from us to put together all other skills we have and need to learn, in order to successfully interact with others. For example, people with well-developed interpersonal skills will never aim to do things their own way if others are involved. They will consider other views and emotions of their peers. By demonstrating cooperative spirit and open-mindedness these people will foster inclusiveness and acceptance.

In order to strengthen your relationships, there are two key skills that will help you improve your interpersonal communication. These are empathy and social skills.

Empathy

Empathy stands for the ability to understand the needs and feelings of individuals and groups, and being able to see things from their point of view.

Achieving empathy does not always come easy, but there are ways to learn it. First of all, listening effectively both to verbal and non-verbal messages, the body movements and gestures.

First of all, observe how you react to people. Do you judge before knowing all the facts? Do you jump to conclusions in the middle of a conversation? To begin strengthening your empathy put yourself in other people's shoes and try to feel their point of view. The path to this is through effective listening — being attentive to what the other person is saying and being involved with their story.

Effective listening requires the people who converse to face each other and let no gadget or task distract their attention. The important thing is — stay attentive. This means being with the speaker fully, preventing your mind from wandering elsewhere. An effective listener is the one who doesn't judge, but instead listens to the thoughts and emotions of another person with an open mind. Avoid jumping to the conclusion or sentence-grabbing — and remember that you're not alone in this conversation. Another no-no for effective listening is planning what to say next and rehearsing your lines when others are speaking.

People's minds wander during a conversation, even if they don't want them to. In order to prevent this, allow your mind to process the words in structures that make the conversation more lively to you, such as — putting words in pictures.

Asking questions is not only a great way to keep your conversation focused, but it also shows the speaker that you care. Giving hints that you understand what they're communicating and are interested in their thoughts will set you on a path of empathy building before you know it.

Another key ingredient to empathy is developing others, or acting upon their needs, concerns and helping them get where they want to be. Being a point of support for another person shows that you frankly care about their life, and you can do this in your own family, among friends or co-workers. Simply begin by giving feedback on something they've done — encourage their hard work, their accomplishments, but also be prepared to offer your opinion on how they could improve in the future.

Social Skills

Humans are highly sociable creatures, and throughout our evolutionary history we have developed ways to communicate our thoughts and feelings, and on the way build strong connections. Being able to easily talk and form connections with others is another way of raising your EI. Socially skilled people who show social responsibility and focus on the development of others (show empathy) tend to attract more high-quality connections in their social circles, while their well-developed social skills help them manage other people's emotions for the well-being of both counterparts.

The term *Social skills* encompasses a wide range of relationship types and interpersonal skills: from leadership, conflict management, working in a team, or persuasion. Some of the skills are rooted in self-esteem and self-confidence. By developing social skills, we become more attractive to others, which increases our social satisfaction. In turn, this goes into a cycle and increases self-esteem and confidence, establishing the foundation for self-acceptance.

Polishing social skills take time and exposure to social occasions. However, there are things you can do every day in order to build advanced social skills for every occasion.

Communication skills are pretty much at the core of social skills. It takes skills such as listening, keeping small talk and building up on common interests to form a relationship with another person. We've covered some key social skills in the previous chapter, when we talked about empathy and ways to develop it.

What we haven't mentioned yet, but is the crucial rule of every interaction is: be respectful. This means, treat others the way you'd like them to treat you, a.k.a. The Law of Reciprocity. It starts from your thoughts — even if you say nice words to someone, the way you behave, the tonality of your voice and body language will speak volumes. Aligning thoughts with spoken words will prove you honest and show that you interact with integrity.

Attitude check is required even if you're not around people. Are you a positive person? This will affect your relationships. Negativity is not bad per se, and life is never just a train of fluffy and happy events. But, there are things we can control, such as choosing to stay positive and hopeful regardless of external circumstances. Instead of seeing problems everywhere, the positive attitude will help you see opportunities and what's good in almost any situation. Start by listing things you're grateful for in your life. Is this your family, your dog, or your car? Whatever it is, make sure you acknowledge the good in your life.

If you've ever spoken in the public, you know that one of the essentials is to know who you're talking to. Even if you're just making small talk at a dinner party, try learning more about the person across from you, so you can have an engaging and interesting conversation for both parties. This is where empathy comes back again: try to keep the other person's perspective in mind when you try to get your message across.

We all rely on fillers to fill the silence while we think our thoughts out, but they're not nice to listen to. Um's and ah's do little to communicate your message, other than portraying confusion and a lack of track of the words. Cutting them out will make you sound more persuasive and appear more confident. A good conversationalist will take their hands out of the pockets, relax and pause before speaking. The silences might seem awkward in your head, but to others, they sound just right.

Emotional reactions

As previously suggested, keeping a journal will help you track down how certain situations make you feel and, more importantly, how you react to them. Your response to a certain condition will influence the way other people perceive you and, directly, how you feel about yourself. People often wonder how they could stop reacting in a certain way: "How do I stop my anger?". But we cannot just simply change one thing in order to make the big change we want to see — there's no easy fix.

Some authors suggest that in order to change emotional reactions we need to think of our mind and emotions as a garden — a breathing and growing field of emotional energy that we plant and nurture to bring to life. We strive to nurture the fruit that will bring us joy, and we want to plant out those that will bring us anger, stress, and fear. Every thing we do goes into our emotional gardens — the way you react to circumstances will plant another seed on your emotional field. What will you choose to plant?

Your garden requires constant tending — eliminating potentially harmful seeds and planting the ones that will gratify you with inner peace, growth, and joy.

In an attempt to help with undesired emotional reactions, some people choose denial as a way to stop the reactions from happening. Or, expressing this in gardening terms, denial and shutting down is the chemical that kills the whole garden, even though you just wanted to kill the weeds.

At the very core of emotional reactions are false beliefs, not necessarily obvious at the first glance. In order to see it clearly, we need to assess it after removing the feeling of victimization of being judged. The victim point of view is attached to low self-esteem, powerlessness, and fear, while the judgment point of view involves being "right", high ego and a habit to criticize everything.

Being in control of one's emotional reactions first requires knowledge that we have another choice. It takes a significant amount of willpower to turn to the alternative, but some exercises can help regain personal power over the emotions. One of them was previously described — imagining situations we expect to happen and jotting down how we expect to react to them. If the imagination is unpleasant, we can work on changing the scenario and reacting the way we'd like to see us behave.

While learning how to control your emotional reactions, be okay with your emotions, even if anxiety, fear or frustration do not subside easily. Accept your emotions, but make an effort to choose how to behave. Taking a note of how your actions make others feel may help you through this — does your anger scare people around you? Does you bursting into tears make your family worried? Going back to practicing empathy will help you determine this, and even though we don't know you, we guarantee that those dear people around you will be happy to see you being in touch with your emotions and handle reactions without drama.

Taking responsibility for your actions will show your acceptance and the willingness to change your ways. If you hurt someone's feelings don't ignore what you did or avoid the person — nothing is more appreciated than apologizing directly.

Conclusion

As previously noted, just by reading this or any other book on emotional intelligence will not improve your life. However, by taking knowledge into action, you have the power to turn your life upside-down. And, what's even better, to turn lives of dear people around you upside-down, too!

This knowledge equals the knowledge of alchemy. Learning how to feel, communicate, express and respond will turn your hours of effort into the gold of openness and happiness. Take care of your emotional garden, and you will receive golden apples in return.